# The Color of Dirt

**The Color of Dirt**
Copyright © 2022 Giulio Magrini

All rights reserved. No part of this book may be used or reproduced in any manner whatsoever without written permission of the author. Published 2022.

Printed in the United States of America.

ISBN: 978-1-63385-465-9
Library of Congress Control Number: 2022914686

*Layout and Design by* Jason Price

*Published by*
Word Association Publishers
205 Fifth Avenue
Tarentum, Pennsylvania 15084

www.wordassociation.com
1.800.827.7903

# The Color of Dirt

*poetry and flash fiction by*

Giulio Magrini

WORD ASSOCIATION PUBLISHERS
www.wordassociation.com
1.800.827.7903

*For my wife Barbara and Nonno Giulio Magrini*
*I breathe their blessings*

# Personal Notes

**Giulio Magrini** started writing poetry in the early 1970's, and takes most of his inspiration from the darker sides of human nature. He has performed at the Three Rivers Arts Festival many times, and numerous other venues in Pittsburgh. Giulio has conducted poetry workshops in alternative high schools, prisons, drug and alcohol rehabilitation centers, and hosted a radio show for local poets. He was asked to perform one of his poems, The Pittsburgher, as an elegy honoring the late mayor of Pittsburgh Richard Caliguiri with the Pittsburgh Symphony at Point State Park before a 4th of July crowd of over 100,000 people. That poem is now archived in the Heinz History Museum. Magrini has always preferred the performance of his work over publishing, until now.

# Acknowledgements

To Vincent Zepp and the Szep Foundation for subsidizing and illuminating local art and poetry in Pittsburgh. The inspiration continues and swells. To the esteemed Viviana Altieri, and her Istituto Mondo Italiano-Centro di Cultura Italiana, without whom I would not have had the confidence to include my work in Italian. To Jana Pail and James McNally, who supported this project as close friends and in substance. Finally, thank-you to the encouraging audiences who supported my work through the years. I am grateful to all of you.

Grateful acknowledgement is made to the following journals, anthologies, and blogs for providing a home for my work: Dumpster Fire Press; Alien Buddha Press; Fevers of the Mind; Ukraine: Night and the Fire; I Ain't Your Marionette Publishing; Rye Whiskey Review; The Writers Club; and Impspired.

**Inspirations for *The Color of Dirt***
The amazing Caridi families of Sharpsburg. My mother was one branch in their sizable tree of righteousness.

Magrini's Tavern, on the corner of Magee and Gibbon Streets, in the Bluff, Pittsburgh, PA.

The families who resided on Voelkel Avenue in Dormont PA. We couldn't be closer.

My mother-in-law Helen R. Heinz, a woman from Bethesda, OH who worked hard all her life. The wonder of our developing respect for each other was one of the victories of our lives.

Clay Boyd, my best friend as a young man who taught me to appreciate friendship. He was one of my important exemplars of manhood through his strength, kindness, and love.

Ron Molinaro, my friend and the owner of Il Pizzaiolo restaurant. He brought Pizza Vera to Pittsburgh, and with it a generosity and kindness that amazes me to this day.

Dormont Borough in the 50's and 60's. The tree-lined streets, soda fountains, parades, and insulation of that one square mile of neighborhood exemplified the shifting, but beloved aspirations of America in the day.

Massimino (Mino) Minnetti, my best friend as an older adult who shared his special cultural knowledge of his original home in Roma and Italy. I carry his sense of humor and cuisine with me in his memory.

My gratitude to the inspirations that tried to teach me as my mind wandered like an indecisive bee around the promises of flowers.

# contents

## I. AMORE (LOVE)

Vince to Rachel Over the Fourth River in November....3
The Pittsburgher................................................................4
We Are Here.....................................................................6
Adequate Praise...............................................................8
Come Accarezzare Il Fiore Della Mia Moglie?.............9
How Do I Caress the Flower of My Wife?....................9
Mating With A Panther................................................10

## II. ARTE (ART)

Artists and the Intelligentsia......................................13
What We Can Do..........................................................16
Chi-Chi Artistes............................................................19
Disregarding the Suicide of Gray Birds.....................23
After All... They are Artists........................................27
Interview with the Man on Cyber Vacuum Island.....31
Gray Sky...Drizzle...It's Not Night.............................33
No, You Can't Write Poetry........................................34
Hong Kong....................................................................36
Sono il Vento................................................................37
I Am the Wind..............................................................37
The Last Butterfly of Summer....................................38

## III. ODIARE (HATE)

Christ Was Crucified Once..........................................41
Turning the Channel from Your Lovely Pose
    to the Hate Picnic....................................................43
Evil Hiss on Infinity Street.........................................45

Discovering We are Extinct: Intro ............................... 46
Discovering We are Extinct........................................... 48
Catatonia and the Complication of the
    Simplest Human Endeavor ................................... 49
Days Slip Away............................................................. 53
Better to be Born an Animal........................................ 58
Saying No to the Passion and Death of
    Frankie Tremé........................................................ 60
No Penance for Masturbators ..................................... 63
Le Mani E Piedi I Suoi Peidi Sono
    Sempre Freddi Dice............................................... 67
Her Hands and Feet are Always Cold She Says........... 68
Not All You Need is Love and I Do Not
    Want to Hold Your Hand ..................................... 69
Reflections on the Exodus from Hell........................... 71
The Dews of Eden........................................................ 73
When the Going to Die Blues Transitions
    to the Going to Die Anyway Rag......................... 74

## IV. POLITICA E GUERRA (POLITICS AND WAR)

Finding Someone to Impress........................................ 79
Kings and Queens of America...................................... 82
The Story of a Man's Heart.......................................... 86
Not Dancing in the Ashes of Dreams.......................... 88
Hitler Could Not Dance or Paint the
    Human Figure........................................................ 90
Voices Along the Roadbed........................................... 93
It Will Be Done............................................................ 95
The Phone Rings Like it Always Does........................ 99

## V. SPORCO (DIRT)

The Difference Between Peering and
  Peeing ≠ "R" in the Key of C .................................... 103
Coolbreeze Bites the Big One at Brewski's ............... 105
My Unclever Poetry or Just Don't Give Me
  the Look .......................................................... 109
City Feces in Snow ........................................................ 111

## VI. FAMIGLIA E RELAZIONI (FAMILY AND RELATIONSHIPS)

Offering for a Princess .................................................. 115
Little Sister ..................................................................... 119
Never Again Nonno: Introduction ............................. 123
Never Again Nonno ...................................................... 125
After the Strawberry Man ........................................... 127
Reflections During the Last Voyage ........................... 131
For Aunt Gloria and the Unfamous ........................... 136
Il Cristiano di Notte Soddisfatto ................................. 137
The Night Christian Satisfied ...................................... 137
Papa Dino ....................................................................... 139
The Speech of Angels ................................................... 143
She was too Young to Know Any Better
  She Called Him Little Friend ................................ 146
La Cara Ragazzazina Toscana ..................................... 148
Selinsgrove Dark ........................................................... 153
For All My Days Remaining ........................................ 156
The Revelation of Her Embrace .................................. 159


The Color of Dirt Afterword ........................................ 161

# I.
# AMORE (LOVE)

# Vince to Rachel Over the Fourth River in November

*For all lovers*

Every time

I love you

A flake of snow
Forms separate
Distinguishable

If in these years
I have surrounded you

In a blizzard of love

You should know

I could not help myself

I never knew
I would love someone

That it would begin every day
And be you

# The Pittsburgher

*A memorial for Richard Caliguiri,
Mayor of Pittsburgh 1977-1988*

**NOTE:** Mayor Caliguiri would at times go home to shave his father, and have lunch.

Behind the glass of sky
Layers of wet
Glisten and descend
From the clouds over
Lawrenceville Morningside
and East Liberty

The morning rain
Tenderly coats
Metal rails
Embedded in cobblestone

Along the banks of the rivers
Steel mills
Become fossils
And a watery clacking of heels
Is heard on North Millvale Street
The calm
Is upon us

The spirit of Richard Caliguiri
Continues
Without pause
In this
Pittsburgh Pennsylvania

The heavens of neighborhoods
Fill the guardian stars
With tenderness

And we feel it

In the corners of his mouth
The light in his eyes
Or as he shaved his father

Io amo questa cittá papa
I love this city papa

The earth grows soft tonight
Stardust coats the alley-ways
Rivers and bridges

We are able to see
The potential of humanity
In the life of
This Pittsburgher
The bells toll
Songs to the eternal
Fill the churches
And it is said

Blessed are the pure in heart
For they shall see God

And we know

# We Are Here

*Have a nice day with anyone you love*

I am he and I will always remember
We are harmony unlearned
Our essence
And the epitome of world
The indistinguishable connections
As we ponder the discoveries
Beyond it

Our caresses are never enough
We consume the Earth
By engaging each other
Everything is the beginning and the middle
We are one white enduring iris
We develop in language and music

We speak the unspoken
And we hear the unheard
The right hand of sharing
And the left hand of uncertainty
Converge upon us
We travel through visions together
Treachery beckons
Certainty shuns us
Truth cannot be trusted
And we are glad
We embrace the unfinished
And so turn upon ourselves
To doubt to question to stay the course

What mechanism isn't this?
There was never a destination
But the cues of the infinite
Batter and multiply

And it is whispered
It is no use to continue

We turn our distracted gratitude
To each other
And alter and compound devotion
To the extremities of wonder

We live in our distorted continuing
And the mystery of us

We are here
We have always been here
And we will be here after we have gone

## Adequate Praise
*For Barbara*

Precipitations of cumulus gardens

Will rain bouquets forever

If a flower

Could shower

Adequate praise of thee

## Come Accarezzare Il Fiore Della Mia Moglie?

Prendermi cura di lei ogni giorno
Nutrirla
Godere dei suoi meravigliosi colori
Respirare il suo profumo
Perché lei ti sosterrà
Fino alla fine dei giori
Dopo i semi del suo fiore
Nutrono la tua memoria
E tutto quello che ha toccato

## How Do I Caress the Flower of My Wife?

Attend to her daily
Nourish her
Enjoy her wonderful colors
Breathe the scent of her
For she will sustain you.
Through the end of days
After the seeds of her flower
Nurtures your memory
And all she has touched

# Mating With A Panther

*(two voices)*

Bitter angels torture her heart

> *Through the certainty of her perceptions*

Translucent skin

> *Bare shadows of sinister mysteries*

Offers ambiguities to be solved

> *By qualified men of good breeding*

Her lips drip Grand Marnier and Kierkegaard

> *He thinks she has chosen*

To sweetly kiss him

> *Her eyelids begin to close*

Imperceptibly

> *Imperceptibly*

Like the footsteps

> *Of a panther*

In the night

# II.
# ARTE (ART)

# Artists and the Intelligentsia

*Pere-Lachaise Cemetery is the largest cemetery in Paris, where Oscar Wilde is buried on Avenue Carette*

Clouds of mystery veil beatified innocents
Sliding on a winding suppressed detour
Stacked with rocks and littered glass

Our apprentices study the boundaries
And decide to investigate beyond the threshold
Initiate a journey to investigate
This indefinable moment
To illuminate and pursue
The passion and work of art

On the meandering path
They behold billboards of distraction
Obstructions in flashing lights and jingles
They hear the fortunate privileged
Ignite the fuse of commercials
Advertising the business of technique
To the sponge of masses

But through the destiny of
Internal aesthetic justice
A wondrous phenomenon of disruption
Explodes unexpectedly
And thunders in recognition
By nomads lost in the wilderness
And the mayhem of world

They are conducted
By an artist's instrument
To the gods of harmony
And the explanation of humankind
The iconic slumbering artists of history
Decay prominently in Pere-Lachaise
Jangle with the breathing collective leftovers
Subsist around mediocrity and sighs
Outcast peculiar
And marginalized

The craft is camouflaged by the intentionally bewildered
Senseless to the possibilities of achievement
And the thunderous truths of the invisible
As they disintegrate and withdraw to obscurity
Exalting the stars with their answers
These mediums these visionaries of civilization
Were defined through history
As an artist's production
That begets the manifestation of us

These chosen few
These artists
Exploring the challenging corridors
Of consciousness
Pursue the natural continual reflection
And expression
Of what it is to be human

Hear the melodies of spirit
Recognize delight and fury
In the blending of notes
Tints of color
And the composition of words
In this concordant and disharmonious world
The intelligentsia
Huddle and execute smug impersonations
Categorize au courant dilettantes
To the innocent and novitiate
Who were not apprised of violence
And the camera is coerced in sorrow
And pans to Avenue Carette in Pere Lachaise
Where the lips of Oscar Wilde
Contort even tighter

# What We Can Do

*Do not let them turn us against each other*

There is nothing we can do
To the overlords preying over us
Nothing we can do
To the governments that suffocate us
Nothing nothing
And more nothing to be done
Our friends sabotage us
We return to our families
Failing to soothe us in our pain
They shower
Combustibles of assurance
Deluged in opened sores
Explosions burning cruelty
And it becomes worse than nothing
Unconsumed fiery apathy
Fiends lurk in every direction
They blind us
And I believe I hear them scream
They bludgeon and prod us
And try to devour our remains
In a blood red wave of engorgement
They are more than hungry
They are malnourished
Hollow fangs hidden behind their lips
We are beaten at their festivals
They are purified by our screams

There is no need for air or the future
Because there is nothing
And nothing to be done about it
Our destruction
In screams and lamentation
Coexists with
Their sweetest contentment

The defamation of our existence
Shapes their paramount joy
Until we are eventually slaughtered
There is nothing we can do
In the remaining void
That is the distillate evil nothing
Not even the smacking of corrupt lips
Heard quietly in the background

There is something we can do
To march forward
Smile at the human hearts
Beating hopefully and in syncopation
On the streets and subways
Tables and beds
And we touch the hands
Of the curious depraved lonely and weeping
There is something we can do
To carry the silence with us
And take it to every being in chaos
Or bring those two hours before dawn
Or any other hour
For no other reason than
They were sleeping

And that time
Should be shared by everyone
Together in the moment
Laughing walking and if necessary
Fists clenched and fighting as one
In the battle for righteousness
Because we are told by the highest authority
Our individual human spirit
That this is what we must do
To live
To continue
To love
And to die

So that this place and these people
Become better
Or to allow access
To the ones not yet here

There is something we can do
There is something we must do
We are beautiful
We are the consummate dawn and dusk
And the life in between
The emergence of mud to the gods and back
In the cycle and the circle of creation
And we are the things that must do
What has to be done
To continue to grow
To love and to share the inner grace
And everything else

# Chi-Chi Artistes

Historical obscurities
Fall from the poet's tender lips
In drops of solemn black rain
Open-mouthed listeners
Stare bug-eyed
Comatose
Scrunch their eyebrows
Do the heroin nod
Blissful smiles portend
An indecipherable clarity of understanding

The disciples
Are under sedation

The poems of icons
Are venerated quietly
In shadows and rows
As the artiste masturbates
Fifteen-watt bursts
Of antiquated mystery and symbolism
Golf applause
Golf applause
Who can appreciate
The mysteries of the gifted?

Watch them slowly now
As they scratch bleeding fingers
Into the stony dirt
To praise truth and beauty

Defined today
As a cloudy day
In the tomb

These trembling mystics
Posture and quiver their art
It is spun to us
This is the language of prophets
And the prisms of the Lord

Within the radiating jurisdiction
Of publicity men
That may be known
As the beat and swirl
Melody and word man
Initiates a brilliant twilight separation
Between those who are artists

*And those who are not*
We are told of their muses
Voices
And foggy peculiarities

They're complex and neurotic
Zealots of the first order
Undisciplined in the use of
Controlled substances

And it is whispered
They empathize
With minority causes

Artists feel pain we can only
Hope to feel

We are apprised
This is the artist's mystique
Oh ladies and gentlemen
Thank you
Thank you very much

I have two special friends
Who close their letters
With the phrase
"In poetry"
How right they are

Everything
Is "In poetry"
Not poets
But people
People who write poetry
Do it because they must

Poetry is their natural continual reflection

Everyone must write because
We are the people and
Our voice is true

# Disregarding the Suicide of Gray Birds

In the former days
Before parades of upgrades selfies
When reality was not entertainment
Gray birds soared under clouds
To the limbs to the nests
In continuity and steady flight
Their melodies enchanted the heavens
Introducing the sky
To the imperfect firmament below
In partnership we witnessed
Elegance grace
Accepted their generosity
In song purpose and passion

Those were rare days
Of secluded memories
When pure and effortless song
Glorified the air
Soared in the skies
With contentment born of harmony
Uplifted in the certainty
Of colors
Luminescent in the heavens

The rain fell
Like any other day
When feathers had shone
In spontaneous passages

No one noticed
The threatening clouds
Rising over the slate gray sky
A murky haze suffocated the air
Monotony and predictability
Were projected in our heavens
Obscured by noise

In the dreary desolate
Days and shadows
Unconditional structure
Replaced renewal of song

Flight became tedious
And there was frightening decadence
Through the widening abyss
Passing in the air
Without vision
Familiarity or understanding

And the suffering of only one
Is not the prerequisite limitation
Of this terrible day
But developed and shared
In violent abandonment

These were the pages
From the story
Of the suicide of gray birds
And the slander of nature

We assess the vacancies of harmony
That have invaded our clouds
Darkened our world
And become the authors
And witnesses
Of our devastation

Observe these charcoaled
Twisted flights of whim

The futility of conflict
Assaults our susceptible spirits
And suggests we concede
To surrender in futility
This unbearable constriction
Attacking our vulnerable hearts

Do not despair my friends
Inside my gray feathers
*And yours*
Are brilliant sparkling colors
That dwell within our spirits
Bequests from those gray birds of old
Whose legacy was passion in time
And growth to lift us
Beyond our grasp

We know the multicolored song
And we will sing it
Even if we are the only
Birds in the woods

# After All... They are Artists

*Those who like to control the world despise artists. They are afraid of the power we wield in a pen, a brush, a photograph, to establish the light of truth.*

They are embraced by the corrugations of lacey wings
What course of flight targets our paths?
Their diet of leaves of plants
Raises them above carnivores
Their bellies are full
Before the infidels can feed their beasts

But they are the hated artists
Scorned by the effete privileged
A swarm of killer writers
Told they can cause major cultural damage
If left untreated
Or introduced to social media
Their inspiration devastates the world
And something must be done

After all...
They are artists

What form of removal
Or self-eradication will purge the obliviates
Artists are the locusts of the world
And they do not even have the courtesy

Of being in-season or scheduling swarms
They are everywhere
And worse
They publish
They lie in the fields of small presses
Chomping on verse and simile
They are told by those who know
And dine with them
That their choices are divine
And they trust the lies
Of their comrades chirping in the weeds
As the corrugations of their wings
Are many and varied

After all...
They are artists

And they live in the patrician fields of our world
Controlling not killing us
An interesting problem
For those who take sport in their fancies

After all...
They are artists

Dangerous, brittle, moody, and worse
Unconventional

**Artists Rejoinder**

We engorge ourselves on your criticism and embrace your scorn. You drive stakes through our language and your own. Take flight from our whims of fancy and glide through the sky using our gifts. Observe the fat cynic last in line as he tries to merge his distaste for us with an understanding of current events. The deterioration is upon you. It will come, and I am wondering who you will turn to...

# Interview with the Man on Cyber Vacuum Island

I am the only one here. There is no one else. My interpreters, these companions... scribble entanglements and the blinking lights display intimacy, and the software connects me with interactions. As I reflect on these flashing links, I begin to feel thinner and sense the lovely embrace of ice. The footsteps I listen to are my own. What I thought I wanted to hear was someone else's steps, but my echo is enough. I do not know where or how to download the sound of other steps. I have organisms in cyberspace. I have my speakers and digital stimuli for the voices for the touch and yes even the smiles. I have imagined the need in their eyes that I can interpret if I know the password and answer the secret question. Otherwise, I remain safe and unconnected.

This is my island of machinery of buttons, lights and blinking screens; my techno android of my design and I am exclusive titleholder. I know what they will do for me. I have a contract with intricate, prescribed terms. We turn each other on when I connect with every other anaerobic workstation, and there need not be negotiation. Do you envy my victories? I do not know the taste of tears and the warmth of a caress of what I am convinced is every potential sorrow. I have seen them on YOU TUBE and the crazed comments of assassins. They breed panic and felony, and I am safe behind my firewall. Yes, rejection is obsolete on my island. They show me paraphernalia I do not need anymore, and reveal it is pleasant to reminisce from the safety of my keyboard.

My love is reliable, contractual, and cannot hurt me unless I click SUBMIT. I am inoculated for sadness and abide in absolute control. You have asked me again and again if it was always so pale here. It is not that I do not notice, it is that I do not want to notice, and do not see the shades you need to see. You pay the price for your colors, your choices, and that is the slow drip of blood seeping imperceptibly from your heart. Do you think these two dimensions bother me? Do you think that I suffer? Do you think I am delusional and secretly want what you try to have, but never grasp? I surf your world my friend.

You are the home of covert monasteries inhabited by corporations that colonize your moments; eharmony.com; the collapse of journalism; and your audacious choice of personalized Steeler jerseys instead of supporting decent education. Your families, communities, and governments cannot agree on the setting sun, and you blame god for the things you are not able to fix. Some of my biggest fans are your children. Look at their eyes as they shimmy from side to side... They clutch at their devices and retract from communication in the moment like lethal disease. They are searching for cozy islands of their own as you watch. Maybe one day they will let <u>you</u> interview <u>them</u>.

You see me living in a lesser world, but I am the one who lives within my parameters and observes my rules, and your criticism of this place is not valid here. Sin no more in your own Eden. Corral your children and bury your murdered dead if they authorize. Do not bring your poison to the perfection of my solitary regulated frontier.

# Gray Sky...Drizzle... It's Not Night

Dusted clouds choke deliberately

Night teases in coatings of gray

Layers of wet glisten slimy

On the fear and brooms

Tin cans whiskey and suspicion

Cyclone fence and glass

On the guns for protection

Coal dust and death

# No, You Can't Write Poetry

If you carry initials after your name
You cannot write poetry

You must first figure out everyone's woke-ness
Achieving perfect symmetry
In an environment of smug confusion

If you are wealthy
Don't you dare write poetry
If you are poor
You can write it
Because you are powerless
And no one listens

If you rhyme
You can write poetry
You will aggravate everyone
Your words a self-fulfilling prophesy
In harmonious contempt

Write poetry that is amorphous
Incomprehensible and perplexing
The vapid will be transfixed by you
And the scholarly will ignore you

Your attempt to occupy
A gloomy or cheerful preoccupation
In poetry
Is pathetic and wretched

Don't waste your time
Poetry is not your thing
It is not meant
For your type of person

And what are you doing
Listening to what you think is poetry?
You live in dissonance with poetry
Plans should be made
Subscriptions cancelled
For anthologies and meds
For you cannot write poetry

You do not belong
With those others who do not belong
For they are the poets
And live in the ether

They breathe the air of the misbegotten angels
Needing to fly in the polluted air
Speaking the language of the dead and dying

But someone has to do it
And the person who is crucified this time
Cannot be you

Because you cannot write poetry
We have poets for that

# Hong Kong

Soft white and pink lotus
Float downstream
Kayagum twang
A rhythm of life
Butterflies
Flip in gardens


A young boy
Contemplates poetry
And affirmation
Is it possible


Glad hearts

## Sono il Vento

Ho già passato questi alberi nudi
Là dove sei.
Hai sentita la mia canzone?
Era breve
E non sempre bella
Ma l'ho scritta per te
Gli alburi nudi
Quando ti trovi tra loro
Non ricordarme
Pensa a me

## I Am the Wind

I passed through these bare trees
You stand among
Did you hear my song
It was brief
And not always beautiful
But I wrote it for you
Bare trees
When you are among them
Don't remember me
Think of me

# The Last Butterfly of Summer

Flutters past my window
Like a Van Gogh strobe light
Vanishes flashing into
Autumn sweetness

Trees cover light
Crimson golden-brown
Crisp leaves fall
Stiff whirl-a-way

The earth grows soft for lovers

# III.
# ODIARE (HATE)

# Christ Was Crucified Once

The rest of us were made to be recidivists
Perspiring fingers slide along beads
There is no resting place for the weary
A miraculous and continuing
Engorged tank of sorrow
Draining the mystery of soul
Assigns an amorphous vagary that holds grace
And fuels your spirit to enlightenment
Advertised in elite journals
By shrewd and consecrated mystics
Contented appeased and evacuated

From baptism to extreme unction
A travail of suffering and penance
Must be tallied
By the most terrible and officious

Auditor in the sky

Greasy haired interpreters
Direct their luminous teeth and thunderous voices

But not always loud...

Celebrants chant in the background
Hymns are sung and there is no doubt
These voices are synchronized with rustling cassocks
Bursting within the sacristy

Enthusiastic and resolute ministers
Benign and solicitous fathers
Swift masters of the soft sale

Despite what you have heard
Or seen in the neighborhood
On the thoroughfares where you live
Not their screaming streets
Or their whispering streets
From pulpits or television amphitheaters

We are their fertile ground of imperfection
The seeds of their ghastly farm
Do not cry
Our guilt is their greatest exploitation
We only need to remember

As we walk through the carnivals
Eating a hot sausage grilled by Mother Mary
Do not be discouraged about your failures
On the ring toss for Jesus
The souls will not be disappointed with you
And the grateful tears at sermon's end
Will not pave your way to paradise

Gauge the satisfaction of your devout collaborators
They taught the pushers their game
Their perpetual currency is repetitive castigation
Love your flaws while you can

# Turning the Channel from Your Lovely Pose to the Hate Picnic

The fatigue of my body
Sighs through my eyes
I am the zealous backslider
Guilty of every offense
Semi-lucid and bungling
Told that I am born to do this

I scrutinize the tenderness
Of your coconut hair
The grit on its shell
And slurp the sour unknown milk
Hidden inside

I am consigned to the
Shortened bus of masculinity
I ride in rainy muted silence
Drops on the window fall and roll
As wet curtains
Weaving through my vision

The riddle of your company
Pursues me
Through your public definitions
I am the sad parade
Forced to proceed before you

Trudging your penance
Not unlike the tedium of menstruation
You are hammered
To the cross of men
Through me

You are deluged with delight
In the sympathy and compassion
Of your sex
While you take the time
To pose for the birdie
And thank all the little people
Who have made our coupling
An audience for your chosen life choice

I scrutinize your performance
Through laugh tracks and screams
We have a winner!
We have a winner!

And you turn with benevolent sweetness
In your puppy voice
And preset smile
So coy and delightful
And proclaim that the husband character
Reminds you of me and you
Laugh and laugh and laugh

# Evil Hiss on Infinity Street

Through the passage of shadows
The wheels clack metallic
On the cobblestones
Of infinity street


Old ladies and hucksters
Eye each other
With hunchbacked suspicion


All they need are tails


They roam

The borders of hell

# Discovering We are Extinct
*Intro*

In the remarkable aspect of time
Grotesque merges to familiar
Infiltrating the caress of phantoms

Pirouettes of lunacy
Straddle the boulevard
Overlords march
In shrouds of patrician pink
To goose-step directives
And pound a tempo
Of bureaucratic chic

I can hear them
Chanting in contentment
While they prey over me

I chirp my schedule
To the numbed associated entirety
And appreciate
That zombies cannot explain my load
Or advise how to discretely carry it
As I continue to converse
With flattened stone

At the very brink of deluge
I am promised anesthesia
Temporary abatement
From the beatings and slander

A kindred spirit promises
That I am alright
And whispers
I will never be alone

# Discovering We are Extinct

I see my rippled image
In the diluted lakes of your eyes
Where is the cleansing of salt
That intermingled between us?

It has occluded inside me
Where it preserves my vitals
Crystalline and dormant
I become the focusing
Through the fog

I remember whimpering promises
Before the bruises and bleeding
But my congealed cadaver
Is displayed in disarray
In a land absent of rainbows

There is no dispensation
In a state populated by the dead
Where the only legacy
Is that the obsolete
Cannot be damaged beyond extinction

We are the undiscovered fossils
Beneath the steps of the living
Dry bleached and lifeless
The memories of our bones
Loiter under the abiding mess
Obliged that no one examines
The failure of our remains

# Catatonia and the Complication of the Simplest Human Endeavor

Masturbation is glorious
A great deal on a used car
Second hand ecstasy
A recurring installment plan
Or a compromise
Breathtaking and magical
Discharged in private
Your rendezvous for damp resignation
Individualized techniques
Of fantasy and compulsion
Through furtive cyber visions
Without the annoying inconvenience
Or the stark and cumbersome nature
Of the sexual workplace

Swing the lights low Charlie

The darkness of night
Is the preferred environment
For the lurking predators
The dazzling tin messiahs
Bearded, grinning, bespectacled
Moneyed, informative, and willing
Displaying outward unruffled charm
From distorted internal tornados
That cannot be predicted

And are not yet available
From the ITUNES store
Listed under the sociopath genre

We characterize catatonia
As a stupor associated with schizophrenia
Characterized by inability to move or speak
Often alternating with sudden outbursts
Seizures of panic
And hallucinations

We declare that it was
Hard to see the attack coming
The philosophy of the wolf
Socially dangerous meat collectors
Divine collegiate righteous
Their passion pocket change
And limp persuasion

Breasts smashed together
Every cleavage an exercise
For the periphery
Plump women drink
As in anesthesia

Seven coats of lip gloss

Bloody smears cross the face

The appearance a manifestation
Of captivity or indications
Of the parasite

Rigid hairs
Cast on heads
Like patè on crackers
Whispering desperados
The shadows soften relentless
WANTED: Victims who believe in myths

Or

Catatonia

# Days Slip Away

You exhale tragedies
Seal doors of diversity
To basic black and a simple blouse
Embellished with hair and lunch appointments
Under the equivalence and certainty
Of being saved

Droning compartmentalized
Satellites
Encircle your frenetic schedule
Supply your honey-less buzz
To the barren and desiccated flowers
That exaggerate your proper geometric garden
Oblivious that the days slip away

You carry the privilege of a woman's burden
Support the nest
And mutter your continuing inventory
Of snide remarks about your vacant ex

Your children have secured and frittered
Socially acceptable professional men
That have given you progeny
We hear bulletins of children
In the background
A droning siren's song
In anxious and damaged pitch

You notice your daughters
Have taken to strange behavior
Which will disappear if ignored
They exhale tersely that
The medication was MD prescribed

It is your mission to understand your role
To imprint the necessary values to the bloodline
Which was written long ago
By bearded dead white men
In an old book you trust

The brown the unsaved
The children of marginals
Do not factor in your agenda
You cannot hear the cries of alternative children
Because you do not see alternative children
Their hunger does not exist
You cocoon in your comfort zone
A small room of your design
The volume not turned up
The colors inoffensive
The food unseasoned

You live with the value
Of the invisible jesus
And your friends who believe
In the invisible jesus
And the insurance policy
The invisible jesus markets

On main street near the starbucks
And the other starbucks

You forward emails
About the deterioration of America
And the attacks from the evil others
You are the Christian white
And the conservative right
Sin is a product of the misdirected

You have not wondered about the time
As the days slip away

There is a fight song, colors
And a flag to salute
And you are very fortunate
To know the cues
To interpret them to others
Who have not seen the light

You know what must be done
To march in the parade
Of the veritable cause
To lay the bricks of the one road
That will lead us in victory
To the destination
That has been sanctified
And consecrated
By the invisible jesus

You lust for the
Blood of the enemy
You can guarantee it with guns
You are privileged to have by law
A bouquet of gun powder encircles you
And mutes the weeping from the eyes
Of those unable to see sons and daughters
Buried by your rights
And the products of your sovereign mission

Gunshots, explosions, rioting, starvation
And the most terrible weapon of all
The unsubtle deprivation of education

You are able to survey the destruction
From the top of your polluted pyramid
And you have not wondered about the time
As the days slip away
And you are not aware

If you are right about the invisible jesus
He will for a nominal sum
Prepare you for a cell
In your whimsical heaven
Where the pedestrian oblivious
Putrefy in detached spirit

Do not fret
He will not condemn or punish you
Punish you
Punish you

Your life of ignorance and sensory deprivation
Has earned you the comfortable rewards
Of blunted stones

No pain will touch you
No pleasure did
Your remembrances of neutral
Will comfort you

You will live in a death map
Where all is outlined
And no chances are taken
No alternatives no colors
No opinions
Just the disinterested promise
Of your disharmonious life
Where your mortal days have finished
And you live in the eternity
Of the distillate of your constraint

## Better to be Born an Animal

*"Civilization will not attain to its perfection until the last stone from the last church falls on the last priest."*    –Emile Zola

This black responsibility
In Wednesday ashes

As our dirty teeth
Caress the body of Christ

Monks cower
Behind the walls
Of cathedrals

The Gregorian chant
Tranquilizes our spirits
Quasimodo strains at the ropes
Of Big Marie
And Gabrielle

We are reminded of rodents
In a skinner box as we scamper
For wafer and comfort

Clouds of incense
Rain blessed waters
On corrupted bodies
Covered in sores of sin

From the ramparts
Below the gorgons
In baritone gravitas and purple vestment
The shepherd counsels the immigrants

Give money to the poor
In St Francis' behalf
He will intercede
Before God

In the night the liturgy
Skulks in the shadows

There is a clanking of keys
And furtive locking doors
Inside the churches
If we are very quiet
We can hear Francis
Giggling through the incense
We can smell marijuana
And hear women moan

Perhaps the English are right
True love is abuse

# Saying No to the Passion and Death of Frankie Tremé

The pain of conversions
Puncture your crown
Dripping red tears
Stream down sallow cheeks
Burgundy tributaries
Remain as ticker tapes
Markers of the devotees
Of your burden

You are the bleating lamb
Bearing the weight
Of the anticipation of eternity
Gethsemane floats in your eyes
As you scrutinize your eager flock
And wonder amusedly
Are they beautiful
because they are perishable
Then die?

Admitting the paradox
That some of these
Carry more eternity than others
You turn to the
Ravishing Magdalene and grin
Deny their strategies for exodus
Of enchanted extinction
And the hyperbole of heaven

A promenade down the enchantment aisle
Yields smoke scapular and medals
To protect you from demons

These heavenly choirs
Continue their unsolicited
Mysterious exhortations
To your bruised bumped
And bleeding followers

This is your obligatory ordeal
For future compensation
Penance like virus
Must be endured
Ping-pong tribulations
Are the sport of sanctification
Your perfect future
Is what is promised


## II.

This continuing mettle
Without a bouquet
At the end of a rainbow
Encourages our solitary hearts
To reach to each other
Without external
Unseen consecration

We nakedly extend our hearts to strangers
Without intimidation persuasion
Or a basket of fruit

Responsibility for every
Action and experience
Is terminated
In flashing caprice
With the end of body

There is no disillusionment
No trumpet blast
Or proclamation
To the people in the street

You are and will be
The distillate of
Stuff to perpetuity
This is the eternal anerobic mess
Of our terminal substance

Cut to the corner of Bienville and Basin Street
Just outside the Quarter on the periphery of Tremé
Sitting on a jazz curb imagining answers
From Being and Nothingness

Slow and Tipitina easy baby
You hear the pleasure and sorrow of the life we know
Sounding sweetly accurate
On the concrete pavement
Thinking that this
RIGHT HERE
Is eternity

## No Penance for Masturbators

*Post coitum ominae tristae is a Latin idiom meaning, "After intercourse there is always sadness"*

The forgiveness of god
Plunges wrinkled hands
Through the confessional
Screams I am a dirty little boy

Stares at my folded hands
As I receive
The body and blood of christ
Imagines alternatives
For their placement

Observe the commotion
Of the methodical procession
And consecrated parade
Of lumpy calloused knees
As they march in obedience
To the infinite calling
Of the celebrant

And the darkened winged angel
Cavorts in his madness
To visit the high traitors of clergy

Attends this snarling collared evil
Ensconced in satin and lace
Embroidered white on white
And the hilarity of extreme unction
Past a weigh station in marble altar
And chalices of gold

We are told that it is the charge of a shepherd
To detail the passage of eternity
Though all is immediately forgotten
When distracted by a
Hershey's with nuts
Behind a boy's zipper

What is the remedy taught in liturgy
For my wretched little soul?
The god that accepts my contrition
Is a basement god
Telling priest rabbi and minister jokes

Ordinary mortals know that
Impure thoughts and actions
Do not equal
Fondling hairless genitalia
Cloaked under vestments and a homily

POST COITUM OMINAE TRISTAE AFTERWARD

I want quantifiable
Not spiritual reparation

I need to be a voyeur and witness
When the cleric's furrowed concerned brow
Gradually smolders and rots
Through the perfume of incense
Burning on foreskin

I need to authenticate
Compassionate smiles
Grinning to maggots
And regulate the torment
Of the benevolent clergy

My charge more complete
Than the custody
Of my mortal soul
Amen

## Le Mani E Piedi I Suoi Peidi Sono Sempre Freddi Dice

Sottile e blu
Il tuo corpo nudo
Corteggia le bufere di neve
Tu esponi il tuo naso rosso sangue
Come una sciabola
Le narici
S'incollano
Con ogni sussulto

Il ghiaccio ti abbraccia
Circonda I tuoi angoli blu
Come un corteggiatore

C'e un leggero brontolio
I denti
Iniziano a brillare
Tu infirierai l'inverno
Per sempre

## Her Hands and Feet are Always Cold She Says

Thin and blue
Your nude body
Courts the blizzards
You expose your crimson nose
Like a saber
The nostrils stick
With every gasp

The ice embraces you
It surrounds your blue angles
Like a suitor

There is a low rumbling sound
Your teeth start to glisten
You will rage winter
Forever

## Not All You Need is Love and I Do Not Want to Hold Your Hand

No cosmetic will correct her interior
The challenge of beauty flatters camouflage


Through glistening teeth and blood-red lips
Her loathing campaign
Trumpets a parade of tainted identity
All instruments played by herself
Blaring off key and vulgar dissonant


No bow
Low enough
Defiled hearts beat quicker at her approach
She is the maraschino atop the masochist
Her gift to those
Yearning for enslavement
Shackled to this posturing needy wench


Satisfy her parasitic needs
As she travels on her nonrefundable road
Because all she ever and constantly needs
Is your love

# Reflections on the Exodus from Hell

Nothing would have the bad taste
To grow over your footsteps

You have degraded from dull mystery
To shrill commercial
And now you pronounce
I am the monster
Waiting in your closet

My tears
Stream down my cheeks
Sanctify my face
In drops of gratitude and resurrection
For you have mistaken
The entrance to the closet
For the exodus from hell

No predicament of a ruthless
And burning doorknob
Will detain me from Eden
Where I am told this experiment
Was created in the first place

My tears no longer
Evaporate in steam
But irrigate and fertilize my choices

They are disconnected
From your heated nightmares
And devoid of the noise
Of your growl and
Extended dripping claws

Reject all hope
Ye who enter here
Stay with me awhile
And let us
Talk of the tyranny
Of reckless choices
And the savagery of the species

# The Dews of Eden

At that precise moment
A perfect red tear
Slides from Eve's genesis eye
And reminds her
Of the dew on the grass
In those first mornings
Outside Eden

# When the Going to Die Blues Transitions to the Going to Die Anyway Rag

They told you
You reached a certain age

Knowing better
A wizened nod
To the assembled onlookers
Growing from the stumps
On the streetcorners
Their glared and cornered peripherals
Noses pointed to the margins
Tracking your regressions
As you falter predictably
An exemplar to the dynamic
Of your devolution

Going through the motions
Biding your time
Until the next big thing

But there is nothing on the horizon
No invitations were sent
No meetings are scheduled
And everything that must be done
Has been done or neglected

The question lingers in the air
What is the point and the purpose of you?

*You see shadows and silhouettes*
*Apparitions of moist tight skin*
*You assailed the unforgiving storms*
*Not giving a damn with her*
*Grinning at terrors*
*They were trivialities to your conceit*
*Vulnerability is your embraced ally*

Smoke stifles your flagging memory
Where the air no longer breezes
The memories pile up unmercifully
Too much to keep orderly
And the chaos and confusion festers
And breeds well in an environment
Of cerebral clutter and noise
Clanging and banging thoughtlessly
Inside your head

The queues are fouled and the memories
Demolished and cracked
The reality of the last beat
Of the measure of your life has begun

We begin our final tune for the evening
*The Going to Die Anyway Rag*
A request by Giulio Magrini

# IV.
# POLITICA E GUERRA
# (POLITICS AND WAR)

# Finding Someone to Impress

**Individual**

It was 105 in Al Fallujah
And he hadn't thought of
Boink-ing Krisi with a K

The images of her face
Were irrational here
And this sandy geography
Had redirected DNA
To another period
Where all things
That went before
No longer applied

In the quiet moments
Before his rapture
He embraced duty
Realizing he is unknown
To home and to those
Who believe they remember him
And the world of allegiance

Swathed in blood
And choking tears
He kept repeating
Please god please
Get me outta here
The name of his savior
Closed his lips that morning

**Universal**

These ordinary men and women
Firebirds in blood
Whistling through the air
They cannot resurrect
The honor of a nation
Or themselves
When soldiers lay
They lay quietly forever
Warriors do not fade to black on a soundstage
But devolve in pieces in VA hospitals

Heed the howling of gladiators
Witness their opaque stares inside sanitariums
Amongst tubes and disinfectant
Death disbursed on the installment plan

It should be written somewhere
That only one horror per person
Is allowable or will be tolerated

This was a foot soldier
Whose duty imprisoned him
To a sandy oven in Iraq

We offer this requiescat in pace
For the soldiers of valor freed under a grassy hill
In a cemetery outside Sharpsburg Pennsylvania

The medals of generals
Sparkle in the sun
And reflect on the sepulchers of the dead
Their rigid salute and the three volleys

Shatter the numbed mourners
And we are assured that honor never dies

Our dead populate rolling hills
And feed eternal flames
The bouquets of sweet-smelling flowers
Caress the crosses and monuments
The romance will never be over
Can the tears quench us?

We know the best way
To honor our dead
Is not to have them killed
But we sustain the administration of war
And we keep the glory that is left
In small boxes and picture albums
To sleep with us
In the darkness of the night
And provide light in the sinister avenues
Of oblivion

# Kings and Queens of America

*For Lady Justice, who we all know is doing the best she can*

All felonies forgiven
Misdemeanors forgotten
Our lungs populated
With cheaters and thieves
Pardons cascade upon citizen villains
We indoctrinate with vacancy
Absolutions incite attacks
The guilty cannibalize their own

Puncture the sky
Poison the land
With no provision for a compass
Everything is authorized

Through these detonations we notice
A solitary statue detailing
The preservation of dignity
The vindication of opulence
It stipulates that we elude passion
The appearance of panic
And by all means
Don't disturb yourselves

Well done thy good and faithful servant
I present this book of law
And evidence of civilization

Platinum and roses await
In the winner's circle
The confident stride of royalty
In magnanimous America
Distributor of dreams and cheap beer
To the unimportant created equals

Cold cash and frozen genders
List the fundamental elements of equation
Occupying a position
Where the soul is thought to be

The dustless cowboys
Purveyors for America's sanitized west
Vaquero garbagemen
Casually embrace their six-shooters
And Sioux warriors grasp the sky
And fall instantly dead
Deaths are portrayed as
Tidy and hygienic
And personify the ecstasy
Of the American process

**II.**
The first lady softly places
A porcelain-colored hand
On her breast
As a guided missile
Erupts into the gentle salt breeze
And frightens the albatross
In the desecrated sky

In our living rooms
Mickey and Minnie
Burlesque happily
They scurry in effeminate fury
To turn America on
And it is an economic windfall
As the kiddies play with the chum
From the Disney company

The morality of acquisition
Suffocates our spirits
And endangers our bodies and homes
She giggles at the lines in our maps
And ridicules our efforts of remedy
Normally an offering
To the hungry eyeballs of politicians
Juggling opinions in the air

We lie in cardiac care
There are no concerned relatives
In the waiting room outside
Sequins glitter on a wet spot
In the middle of the bed
No one is saying anything
The woman with hooded eyes
Smiles appreciatively
America told us she was justice

# The Story of a Man's Heart

It is covered with the glue of cobwebs and pollution decays over it. It is mystified at the crossroads. No one has posted signs, because it is said some things are not meant to be found. The air is stale and it will be stale tomorrow. You see buttons and switches, and nothing is labeled. You push and pull the levers and push this control and that. It does something as you watch. You push the buttons again and pull the swivel to the left then the right and something different happens then different again. And you hear the poets talk of the voice of the winds, the stones, the trees and add representations of such matters as a man's heart. You listen... And no one is saying anything. You listen to this silence thinking it might mean tranquility, but you learn it has moved to another part of town. If it were not for infections and loathing, this man's heart would reside in a vacuum, but technically, there is life where the heart of a man is thought to be. It sits immobile focusing on objects speeding by... Their rush and avoidance is purposeful so that this beating melancholy occupies only the peripheries of their vision. The Old Testament counsels believers to ignore this heart of man, lest they be turned to pillars of salt, and be objectified with the stuff of legend. This heart is outcast and alone and we are better off. Nothing touches it, and no one wants to see or hear it, as the dialogue of a man's heart is impossible, for it is primitive and vile. This is what we are told by the victimized. You might say this condition is justice for the sins of a man's heart. Many consider the irony of perception by the ignorant, that they may characterize this clanging immorality as "heart". A curious anomaly...

What can be done about the heart of a man? It wheezes and struggles erratically. Its arrogant interference, its profane interruption... disrupts the flow of our plan. It is not in sync with who we are and what we want to become; what we need to become. It is therefore anathema to us and should be consigned to the dust, to the rust, to crank and shudder sin, segregated and apart from our contemporary world. The essence of this heart of a man is transgression and we should incarcerate it as we would any criminal.

And so, the order is given and the funds are appropriated for prisons erected for the purpose. We must barricade ourselves against a man's heart that we may advance in the purity of the cause. There must be no interference with our reasonable institutions, and we are told this through repeated promotions by the media and other reliable sources. We are relieved that this disagreeable heart of a man no longer interferes with us. We are grateful to resume in the channels of vacancy. Yes... Resume this protocol as it is in fact an historical continuation.

Before most of you were born... (They usually skip a generation for practical purposes) We hunted the heart of a woman. We stalked them like animals and kept them as trophies. You are too young to remember. This man's heart, this insecure fool, readily assisted us, and now we have completed the project to eradicate this heart of a man. We are left with the purity of a convenient, heartless void. Sweet emotional nothingness. And we stare into each other's eyes and see murder. It is an action of galactic simplicity. There is so much less here; less to decipher; and less to appreciate. We thrive to a convenience of malignant cancerous vacancy, unobliterated by tears, surrounded by smothered joy. I have searched and searched for someone to thank, and a place to go, but I can find no one, and there is no place.

# Not Dancing in the Ashes of Dreams

Unable to dance
They slosh
Trudge in the ashes of dreams
The pace inexorably withdraws
Backwards

Cruel voyeurs

Examine deteriorating
Expectation's limp and gasp
Clutching the golden years

And the LPN asked

What was it this time?
They stretch desperately
Reach for recollection
Embrace the retrospect
And see the bygone dances

We told them that
If it were ever thus
And they had noticed
What was present
Where had they been?

They continue adrift
Through the cognitive fog
Cuddling the images

When they emerge
And vanish in the clouds
When they disappear

Ponder the frustration
Of everyone
Outside their dance
As there is no pleasure
Caressing the dead

# Hitler Could Not Dance or Paint the Human Figure

*(two voices)*

A regiment of ghosts

    *I tell you people*

Tortured ghosts

    *We are loyal Germans*

Stacked limp piles

    *My family*

Atrophy pieces

    *Is not political*

Catastrophe

    *These people*

Auschwitz burns

    *Are not criminals*

Continually

    *They are merchants*

Continually

> *Where*

March

> *Are you taking*

Continually

> *My children*

Forever

# Voices Along the Roadbed

Was that a faint sobbing in the background? You turn your back suddenly and hear what sounds like the changing of channels on a radio. No matter. You turn again and get those pariah glances as you fumble down the roadbed. I can find no home in the rails. I don't know what comfort is, but my wandering in this desolate place echoes my uneasiness step by godless step. I move further down the line, and the destination fixes on the horizon, and remains unchanging as I lurch forward, continuing to traverse the ties.

After winter, winter follows, and winter threatens after that. Bitter rails are embraced by external ice and internal indifference or is it, internal ice and external indifference? Their frigid metal never warms to my traveler's touch, and it does not answer the petitions of other haggard residents balancing their narrow journeys through the diameter of roadbed. There are no comforting slogans or motivational gimmicks blocking the cirrus clouds because a nonrefundable person has no disposable income. Everyone is equally lost under the culture and the economy that represents it. Laws were not created for the scroungers like us. The only commodity is the growth of vacant opportunity, like weeds, and the citizens of the rails carry lost appeals in empty pockets. This is the place that has been abandoned by promise, and there is no expectation of an ending. We are the dust that blows and the smog that settles in the minds and hearts of the disenfranchised. What is the history that lies amongst the rock and the rail? It rejects us tolerably, and we continue on, because our dull intent is to continue into oblivion, regardless of what waits for us there. There is no soundtrack to our backdrop because we have grown deaf through the continuing frozen landscape of the roadbed. Many like us have trod along this brutal frontier. We feel the stones against our soles, and wonder who has felt the rigidness before us. There is enchantment in traveling without direction or knowing why. Each step that is taken provides a confirmation of the reciprocal message engrained in the rock along the rails. This is the never-ending road for those consigned to wander here, and there is no rest behind the bars of this destination.

Who carries the responsibility for this penal environment? There is no myth or creature that is responsible, no imagined creator to construct this travesty. Only one being would rain terror on itself. It is one that would rip the soul and expunge every dream in terrible progressions of destruction.

Those that walk along these rails know that there is nothing to fear under their beds, and that no evil spirit compels them to this stony corridor. It is the fear that lives within, not the horror of an environment too terrible for habitation. Every traveler who ventures here does so with the permission of their personal self-loathing.

Yes. This is where they want to be. This is where they believe they deserve to be. And so, they endlessly walk along the rails and the stone and ties, in a twisted preference of hopelessness. This is not the road less traveled, but the crowded road of the victims of the suicide of spirit. The trains are gone, but the ghosts remain.

# It Will Be Done

*Consume this fast. I wrote this after one of my readings here in Pittsburgh at the Three Rivers Arts Festival*

It will be done
In the middle of the night
Raindrops sting your naked bodies
It will be done
Not giving a damn with her
In the hot sweet rain
It will be done
With glistening wet fingers
Lingering flipping rose petals
It will be done deep
Desiring her trembling body
Like a selfish infant

It will be done
And done again
Praying for money
Green vipers
Pyramids with eyes
Eyes that reveal
You may be nothing
It will be done
Whispering evaluating
Muttering plodding
Climaxing in visions
Grasping the neon vacancy of sex

It will be done like an animal
Crying in the night
Searched and stripped
Washed and sprayed
Put away from the rest of the world
It is done and done and done
And they will not stop

It will be done
By innocents in middle school
Slurping goofballs bennies and ludes
Brown bag lovers sucking sucking
Praising oblivion
With black-eyed smack-eyed
Susies and Jimmies
Unconscious
In the corner of the playground
It will be done and done by them
They will say they will dig it
And a child will prophesy
That it will be done
By doctor death for kicks
By doctor death for kicks

It will be done
To each other
Behind locked doors
Hiding under the bed
Burning bodies
It was done

No one knows why
**Though they think they know**
It is still done
And they cannot stop

It will be done
In nuclear family soup
Lawns
Peanut butter
Disneyland
It is done while the kiddies
Pound and demand and scream
For happy meals

It is done feeling chills
Shuffling to church
Blaming accusing
Perpetuating lies on wedding days
It will be done
Wondering what art has come to
At the Three Rivers Arts Festival

It will be seen
It will be heard
It will be felt and smelt
Right here right now
By you in your life

# The Phone Rings Like it Always Does

The phone rings
**Like it always does**

My distorted reflection
Coats the surface of a refrigerator bulb

> *Mother's heart bangs and shudders quietly*

I turn on the television
Adjust the recliner to the right position

> *Her head smashes against the bathroom floor*
> *The sound of flesh-covered bone*
> *As it strikes rigid useful tile*
> *Is clear and natural*

I can block commercials
On Jeopardy
With the mute on the remote

The phone rings
**Like it always does**

> *Father's brain explodes gelatinous*

I mow the lawn
Not a cloud in the sky
I mumble what a nice day
Though no one is there

> *His head falls to the pillow and twists left violently*

The phone rings
**Like it always does**

Birds in the back
Fly and peck and
**Listen to the ground**
I have a craving for pizza

But the phone rings
**Like it always does**

Who is it this time
There is no preparation
Or explanation
The phone will ring
**Like it always does**

I have taken to staring at its voice
And my vigil of twisted screams
Follow me in my room of silence

**Beware the uncontrollable telephone**

In its psychotic delight
It will clang introductions
To sadness and despair
Heartache and misery
Its frightful sorrow will change you forever

**Don't pick it up**

It spreads nightmares

# V.
# SPORCO (DIRT)

# The Difference Between Peering and Peeing ≠ "R" in the Key of C

*Territoriality refers to any sociographical area that an animal of a particular species consistently defends against con-specifics (and, occasionally, animals of other species)*

The men's room sonata begins...
With dismay I mutter
They make us spray in the same place
No damn alternatives
To this furtive and solitary function
Coerced to perform in this cloistered venue
We enter our asylum
Wary that non-specifics
Masquerading as specifics
Prey in this place

Peripherally acute bladders
Thankful for the fragrance of urinal disinfectant
The blasé penile exploration
The interference and disorder of pubic hair
Our inalienable right
To widen our stance
Lest we fall over from the weight of
An unreliable and unpredictable pendulum

Then the liberation of blessed waters

For me a memory of a long-ago jet stream
Now the citron fountains of Trevi
Needing a spigot
But it is an emotional moment

Screening the possibility
Of moist discharges in my dainties
I close the pearly gates
And purge my evidence

We pray that this melody
Will be continued
A cappella
In contentment and tranquility
When our crooning needs
Emerge in a solitary refrain

# Coolbreeze Bites the Big One at Brewski's

He was undisciplined
In the use of controlled substances
The bartenders called him
Dirty white vulture
But whada-ya-have to his face

He smiled without reason
Through a patina of Brylcreem
And wafting leaded gas
Coolbreeze perched on a stool
At the end of the bar
Supplemented by the fragrance
Of stale beer and urinal disinfectant

He would slouch backwards on his seat
Basking in the hue
Of vertical green patterns
Representing the terminal status
Of a Mitsubishi rear screen
As venal shadows
Consecrated his pasty face

Everybody was continually reminded
Coolbreeze did time

For something horrific
Unspeakable
It made sense
Not to ask for detail

He referenced the joint
Like an intimate and comfortable sofa
His tattoos were threatening
To illustrate the danger within
Women surrounded him
Like malfunctioning space junk
For filthy chic

Coolbreeze was an outlaw
Driving an alabaster sedan de ville
Spiritually undetectable behind the wheel
An ECSTASY license plate
Cracked muffler

But christ...
It was a caddy

His style radical Waylon Jennings
With a wandering southern accent
An embarrassment
To the confederacy
But appropriate to his
Ambridge, Pennsylvania roots

His jokes were finite
And repeated like a zealot's rosary
Punctuated with a wheezing laugh
And followed on the downbeat
By the bar's
Giggling Greek chorus

No one was disappointed
Or surprised
When the laughing disgrace
Spread the word that Coolbreeze
had been wasted

Taken by a disrespectful punk
Wandering the streets for
The low hanging fruit
Of the drunken twilight scene
In the garden of the semi lucid

It was a craven thud from the rear

That slew Coolbreeze
In that alley under the
CUIDADO MIRE POR DONDE CAMINA sign
That callous blow seized green Mitsubishi patterns
From his face

Waylon, Wild Bill, and
The baddest convicts
That didn't make it

Had remained as pallbearers
To the forever bar
Where we know there is no tab

And the stories are sad
But end funny
Here everyone buys
And the inside
Is on the outside forever

# My Unclever Poetry or Just Don't Give Me the Look

Begging apology my submission
Knocks clumsily at your door
Rat-a-tat interrogatives follow

I offer this droll rejoinder
In lyrical form
To the sponge of cerebral linguists

Flashes of suffering
Weary listening
Follow with patience
And excruciating tolerance
To unartful and greedy word-roaches
Scampering in chaos
Through darkening vibrato pages

Just after the propaganda of emoticons
And creases of exclamation
I get the nodding looks

The horrific and pitiable glances
Dreams of flaming purgatory
The burning and flashing teeth follow
Glisten and await
At the expiration and tether
Of my articulations

The poem got the look

A cuddly dependent puppy
Whimpering embarrassing public howls
Would not conform
And they left the poop
For all to see or step in

I got the look as my poem
Receives whiffs of farce
Louie Normale assessed
By the Maraschino select
My weak retort a sneaking toot
To the tedious elite

Somewhere an ethereal florist
A splendor broker
Will populate my latest indulgence

Housebroken by now
In virtuosity ornamental and complete
With illusory whims uncommon in plebeians

My shit will be so good
It will be incomprehensible
Advancing the mission of art
To the obscure or dead.

# City Feces in Snow

A symmetry of icy snowflakes
Caress the heat exuding from my face
A crunch of a monster
Follows my footsteps in the snow

A blinking yellow light
Hums at the intersection
The chains on the salt trucks
Harmonize with the buzz of the walk sign
And massage me to winter twilight awareness
I am one with the wind

I rest in the port authority shack
And listen to my companions of winter
Narrate their February story

As I rest
I notice a beautiful turd
A brown double helix
Piercing the glistening saltwalk
Escorted by satellites
Of dead cigarette butts
Scrutinizing its geometric majesty
Of natural wonder

What conferring rectum

Presented this momento for me

To share accompaniment
Through this port authority confessional?

And the blessings of my comrades

Smile upon me this night
As the bus approaches
The materials of covert elimination
Celebrate the gifts of winter

# VI.
# FAMIGLIA E RELAZIONI
## (FAMILY AND RELATIONSHIPS)

# Offering For A Princess

*Written for my wife Barbara on her birthday 9/11/2002, one year after the 9/11/2001 terrorist attacks in New York City*

You will remember
This was the birthday
I did not pledge my love to you
For you have it
You have carried it with you
Like a rock a razor a rainbow
And you will have it tomorrow

And so I have been searching
For the passage
That would guide
This presentation to you
But as with many treasures
The maps are obsolete
Numbers are unlisted
The party has moved
Left no forwarding address
Leaving vacancy without details
And no keys to locks
Have been found
On any day or minute or moment

You would have thought that this gift
Is like the past reminders of living love
That have trudged marched scuffled and skipped
Through our celebrations together
And you would be right

The rarity of today's offering
Is a conspicuous presence in time
In this globe of human fragility
And juxtaposition
Breaths of wailing
Celebrations in light
Glances of indecision

But not a glance really
An examination in stone and wonder
The consequences resultant
From the attempts that befall
These moments in our hearts

And we hear the song of muted justice
From the gorgons overhead

And in this bleak unraveling of time
I wonder

Why not Barbara

And so my dear princess
I approach you with the timidity
The uncertainty of a child
Filled with doubt but hope

For today I bring you
The wish of peace
That you may know it
And share it with me
Like the rest of your life

# Little Sister

I remember the feel of your candy cane jammies and the lights of joy exploding from your face; the long brown hair was the color of dirt where anything can grow, particularly my heart. It cascaded in confused curls around your shoulders, and like all kids you paid attention to none of it. You were a goddess and knew everything there was to know. And the happiest I could ever be was to be your defender, and teacher, but they called me brother. I would hold you in my arms and protect you from harm. Your trust in me was my license to tease you. You would endure every discomfort because it was I who was the torturer and you felt you were safe from everything. I was not strong enough though, for chocolate icing on birthday cakes, which easily conquered you by surrounding your smiling lips like a clown. These were the days of automatic innocence and happiness. You would forget these days like too many others that elevated our childhoods. I do not know why you forgot me. There was only a remote chance I would understand your growth. I would not, like all big brothers that grow obsolete, remain able to be "big" forever. I withered into your oblivion as a tired reference as you grew older. That was a condition that I would have been able to accept. I would be the person who represented the past tense, and an old barometer of history. You kept the old pictures of our youth, but you did not keep me. I felt your anger. I knew that I was the enemy. I do not know what treaty I broke, and what my offenses were to feed your hatred. You would rail against me because you would tell me and our family that I was a traitor to our parents. You seemed to believe it, and to this day I do not know what you meant, even after our parents have gone. Now, I stand here watching the scrolling pictures that you kept instead of me at the funeral home. Who was this other family, these clusters of strangers smiling through their packaged grief? They nervously extolled virtues that might have been fact or fiction, but the certainty was that they and their stories of you were unknown to me. I was the bereaved stranger, unfamiliar with the history of my family and the stories they tell in the funeral home parking lot. I did not know who you were and how you became that person. I was the brother who was put outside the arms of your embrace.

I have wonderful memories over 50 years old of the kid you were, if only for a very short time. I loved you so much that I could not bear to stop trying to get you back through the discord of years. These recollections of tenderness are stronger than the seeds of hate you planted in your home of isolated fields as you grew older. The conundrum is that your dead crop continues to flourish while your body decays into dust. Your dead hate has a strong life and I am the anima. I am alive with my pain to remember the love we had that was pure and unsullied by the terrible distractions of your growth. You became a mystery while you lived, choosing denial of me rather than acceptance, or even apathy. You chose not to share yourself in life, almost the same as now, still and lifeless. You are no longer able to ignore me, and you would think that would give me comfort. I could dwell on the loss of you as a sister, and that would be true. Our past love is not a bigger truth than your hatred that is remembered through me. It is a nobler truth, or at least a truth I can now live with. Never rest in peace. Try to live in peace, my memory of my little sister Joycie, even if it is a lesson learned too late.

# Never Again Nonno

*Introduction*

It was Friday and the first-generation Italians from our neighborhood assemble at 2957 Voelkel Avenue to visit Nonno. I remember the urgency of their speech, even though I did not completely understand Italian as a boy. I remember giggling when I heard them say the Italian word "più" a great deal. Later I was taught that it means "more", and as I grew in age I always wanted more. These men, who had their hearts embedded in two countries knew what I was to want. They understood the problems of più. "Abbiamo bisogno di più soldi per la nostra famiglia, Giulio" We need more money for our families Giulio.

There was always a gallon of wine that was the product of every year's tradition kept in the wine cellar downstairs. The four-ounce fruit glass and Momma's frown was for me. There were little kids and big kids on Voelkel Avenue, but I was the only little kid drinking even watered down wine. I think Nonno got more pleasure from watching me drink it than I ever got from the taste.

When the peach tree in the back started dropping leaves Nonno painted the trunk with some stuff that looked like white paint. Later Papa needed to cut the tree down which gave us more room to play. This was a treatment designed for Tuscany, not the rolling hills of Western Pennsylvania.

Nonno's bedroom smelled of Ben-Gay. I was a typical spoiled kid who didn't like the smell of liniment and old ways. His pictures remain to remind me of this Toscano who came from Chiesina Uzzanese in 1901. He was attacked by those who called themselves freeborn. They stole his money and tried to take his pride as they did with many of the immigrants. Nonno succeeded for us and provided our home. He smiled through all of it, until my sister Joyce found him dead on the bathroom floor.

They laid him out at Beinhauer's Funeral Home, and I and my four cousins played tag in the rooms, until they caught me in the bathroom, where we all started to cry. We didn't know why we wept then. We know now.

His voice has become stronger through the years, and he continues to share with me. I hear his accent, strain for "più", drink his wine and yearn for the hem of his cloth. I see him in my memory in front of a ramshackle building in the Bluff in Pittsburgh Pennsylvania. Sei l'eternità Nonno. Ti amo...

## Never Again Nonno

Tiers of flowers
Will not take
Powder and rouge
From his cheeks

Scent his breath

With whiskey and wine
Create a scritchy face
To sticky hands
That reach from below

# After the Strawberry Man

The strawberry man was eighty-four. Every morning his Chesterfield chant was heard above the clatter of his cart on the cobblestones. His donkey ambled down Pride Street to McGee and Gibbon. His strawberry travels were part of the daily rhythms of the neighborhood. His jingle was the music of the day, and his wailing serenade through the dew was a sign to the neighborhood that they belonged in this place.

This was the morning of his death, when his broken strawberry chant shattered the April dawn. His fractured wail was his last morning interlude, and closed his life. The sound of his body hitting the cobblestones was the call that suspended commerce and tranquility that day. His motionless silhouette against the cold gray Belgian block made sense in the neighborhood that morning, and a perfect and final conversation was initiated between the stilled strawberry body and the lifeless stone, that attracted the snooping voyeurs. The locals buzzed around the scene, like foreigners in a strange land trying to understand a culture they did not want to appreciate, and whose language they did not recognize. Their eyebrow wonder and spectator perspective were exactly where they wanted to be.

Everyone who was brought up in this rocky neighborhood knew that you do not touch what you do not know. Death provided them with the comfort of ignorance. When you eat your strawberries here you remain grateful, and do not question the uncomfortable queries of the eternal.

Two men roam the old man's kitchen. They are the strawberry sons. In the spirit and time of death they are appropriate and predictable. The units of measurement that day were furrowed brows, mumbling half sentences, and uncomfortable pacing in the kitchen. The smell of masculinity and grief is stifling. One had come from his job at NYU.., a teacher. You know how they are... Honorable, yet ambitious with their lesson plans. Not unlike Caesar, crossing the Rubicon without respect, and home for death again. He was not like the strawberry man. The family reviled his attempts to adjust. It was true that no one could truly understand the cobblestones, but they were the footprints of the neighborhood, and it was easy to see that he was uncomfortable walking on them. He had abandoned the family for a corduroy sports coat with those stupid fake suede patches. The bystanders understood his motives, and were offended with the strangeness of his manner. They resented him and his intrusive ways. There was no allowance in the cobblestones that measured the pain of a professional home for death.

The other son was a pudgy little dog in a cheap brown suit that might have fit one day. He was unevenly shaved, and his part looked like a back road in a map. He also had one of those clip-on bow ties that little kids wear. Women in the neighborhood would say that they trusted one man to teach the kids, and the other to play with them, but not to do both.

There was an old man sitting at the table, sipping anisette. He looked peaceful, almost happy. He had the knowledge of strawberries and cobblestones in his eyes. It was the moment after the funeral, the pain, the tribulation, and the amenities. It was the moment when people asked themselves what they are going to do with their feelings, with his house. It was the moment when life is evaluated and divided, like strawberries in little green baskets. Each son's eyes burn silently into the other. "Why is this man dead?" And they immediately blister back, "Where were you when I needed you?" The indictment of life is in the air. The blazing sorrow smolders strawberry hearts in an instinctive catharsis. They radiate to the realization that the strawberry man is dead, but the strawberries kept growing. The strawberry man had died, but the strawberries didn't stop. The teacher thought it advisable they stop. The one who played with the neighborhood children thought it would be a nice, considerate thing. They did not know that the strawberries will stop. They'll stop when they are ready.

# Reflections During the Last Voyage

**INTRO**
And I hear the voices of the wind
In the sails of the mizzenmast
The frigate caresses the stillness

Great wings stretch from the hull
Into the clouds of glory
Where the sagacious long beards
Squint and mutter
As they review my obedience
To the dictums of the lord
I gaze at my life
Thundering in visions through the skies
The curtain has closed after me
I am overwhelmed
With the roar of nothing
And I question
The meaning of this
I know I am ended
But I am not certain my end
Is the finish

**I.**

I remembered initial lumps of fat
Crawling on a throw rug
Drooling in a highchair
Mystified by the growls
From the giants overhead
I stream rolling tears
And present a fleshy wail of fear
To the grimaces above

**II.**

The smell of a soiled baseball
The perfume of dirt grass and DNA
Tangled in the leather and stitching
Connects me to every kid
Playing inside the laws of the game
There can be no greater triumph
Typified by these scents
They enhance my focus
And the protostar of life
It triggers explosions
Of immature light
Encouraged in those days

**III.**

My loathed gangling
Uncoordinated mess of tissue
Birthing sex and disoriented behavior
A disarray of hysteria and panic

The penance of puberty
This adolescent scourge
Disguised as a gift

**IV.**
Then the ensuing sequence
The pairing and the beating
The affirmations and slanders
The victories and the fiascos
I stride erect in adult supposition
The credulity of life flows through my beliefs
Like a cyclone through a house of cards
I stand in absurdity
Through the wagers of my life
For a great unprepared mystery

I emerge at a time of bleeding and consumption
They gave me one blueprint
And my unbuilt house did not reflect
On the soundness of the plan
Or suggest alternatives for shelter

These were the hungry days
Before the onset of choice
In a compulsion to invite corpulence
To the collisions of my life

These conflicts stimulated
Comfort and a craving for regularity
Not the offerings of diversity

I was the obedient two-legged reactive
Standing sitting clapping smiling on cue
I clearly remembered the intelligentsia
Scolded Amadeus
"Too many notes"

**V.**
I am left with the sum of my feedings
A stew of gossip and blather
That has simmered forever
In the pots of incarceration
From recipes in the kitchens
Of church and state
I may have come to this moment sluggishly
Or in a flashing instant of caprice

**VI.**
I am in the beyond
There are no written laws
To protect me
Or escape from
No craving for war
Collaborator's joy and despair are vanished
They are on a road I no longer travel
I marvel at the disappearance
Of the bars of human love and community
Through penitentiaries of life
Now transferred to my present
Freedom of isolation
I wonder at the shallowness of liberty
When there is nothing to be freed from

The threat of foreboding mystery
Has disappeared with me
And closes with this vestige of ship

**CLOSING**

I begin to fade in progressions
Darkening shades of gray towards black
And absorb the entirety of spirit
Draining into space
Becoming the nothing
And the perfect ending
Of my beginning before the womb

# For Aunt Gloria and the Unfamous

Her life not measured in canvas masterpiece
Celebrity media intimates
Politico assurances after a poll
The flags were not raised
Or lowered to regard her
There was no need for urgency
To respond to the call for help
On Locust Street

She was the wobbling walk
Of drunken red hair
Told me you understand
Don't you
Aunt Gloria needs a drink

Her obsessions were
Scarlet lipstick hastily swabbed
With Four Roses and valium
Then a silly muddling smile

You did not hear on
The six o'clock news
That Gloria is dead
Your soap opera not interrupted
Programming continued on that day

She was the drunk
Down the street
Poor Freddie's wife
Gloria the unhappy person
Like so many others we know

## Il Cristiano di Notte Soddisfatto

Dio ti punirà
Ti punirà
Come punisce me
Cercalo
Negli oscuri passaggi
Rannicchiato là
Sotto le coltri
Che sgorgano dai tuoi occhi

## The Night Christian Satisfied

God will punish you
Punish you
Like he does me
Watch for him
In the dark passages
Crouching there
Under the covers
Flowing from your eyes

# Papa Dino

**Intro**

I remember the day my Nonno died, and I came bounding home from grade school and gave Papa a big hello as I burst through the door. He was at the kitchen table cutting vegetables for soup, and simply uttered "Your Nonno is dead". I looked at him and stopped, unable to react further. The soundtrack of my mother's sobs from the cellar confirmed his statement. Later, I was to write a small poem about the event called:

## Dino's Tears
Dino cut vegetables for soup
His tears have always been delicious

Papa Dino did not recount memories of the USS Silverstein in the Pacific. Was that reverence hiding, or the fear of a fighting sailor in WW II? He was a quiet unsmiling man, managing daylight or night turn at Magrini's Tavern in Pittsburgh. The relatives would comment about his John Garfield pompadour and good looks. He alternated shifts with his annoying brother Freddo, the childless gambler, but there were no complaints from Papa.

Papa hugged children only when they were little. Attention displaced affection, and I could not tell the difference. We knew what was right and what was wrong and the knowing was love enough, even when it was discipline. The absence of hugs did not leave an emotional scar. Although I am told by professionals that people like me can be damaged by lack of affection. I consider Papa's affection a different color, equally valid and valuable to me. I am firstborn and named Giulio after Papa's father and I stand as witness in the court of the heart where no testimony can overtake our watch.

He was on the sidelines when I played football. I cannot picture his cheers because he would not cheer. It would be garish and unseemly to Papa. There was the time he knocked out some kid with one punch, who had hit one of our players illegally during the game. He shouldn't have done that, but I was still proud of him that day, and my teammates were impressed. He stood up for us.

He did not like to call attention to himself, and would not tolerate bragging from Mama or anyone else in the family. He would explain that he was not educated and I would love him more for it. I knew he was explaining that he appreciated and understood things, but he was smart enough not to waste his time on trivialities.

He carried the lessons of Nonno his father through our house and showed us what respect looked like. Part of the reason I admired him was that I believed essentially that his answers were endured and I could follow. My mistakes would not matter because I would fix mine as he had fixed his.  In those days the guidelines were not created with an eye towards attention, care and individual emotions. The rules took precedence and those that disobeyed were outcast and marginalized. Any television show taught us that lesson, if we didn't have Papa. We all wanted to conform with everyone else. There was no greater punishment than to be peculiar.

Papa Dino was the type of guy that the uncles loved to talk to because most felt superior to him in what they thought was a loving way, that you might reserve to a favorite collie. It was "Hey Dean" this, or "Hey Dean" that. Mostly about stuff they knew he had the answer to like: BBQ sauces, booze, or the best way to make tripe. He loved to drink Canadian Club but I never knew him to be sloppy. He smiled to excess when he was drunk which was a dead giveaway, also supplemented by my mother's stern, terrified and stony face riding in our turquoise and white Olds 88. Her nerves were lousy to begin with.

Dino's aging was accompanied by Type II diabetes, which did not go well with his dietary lifestyle. His Sinai inspired commandment that anything in moderation makes sense if we have restraint in mind as we over-ate didn't work well for him.

Towards the end Papa Dino turned grouchy as the pall of Parkinson's disease overtook what was left of the John Garfield looks. He complained that he had become a pill popper. Pills made Papa less human, and in his mind rendered him a lesser creature.

Papa Dino was a veteran who never spoke of veterans or his service. Papa Dino loved to talk about work but hated to talk about how well he was able to do it. Papa Dino, who was the quiet husband and father of four, one boy, and three girls. There was no change in his behavior to my sister who had Down Syndrome to the day she died. He did what needed to be done. He did his job and stood watch every day of his life, now forced to pop pills. This indignity caused him panic attacks. It was not from the pills, was it? It is never one thing for any of us, but for Papa it was the cumulative chips and damage that occur from every moment in his young life on the Bluff in Pittsburgh PA. Always and forever outwards, helping his father Giulio with his business to volunteering for the CCC's before the war and the US Navy during it. He was not a hero. Papa Dino served his bride Ellen and family until his body failed him. He is gone now and will not serve again but the products of his service are here. We can say that we wished he would have taken some time to spend on himself, rather than all the others. Papa Dino did not, but he made that decision and that is all a person can ask. To make their own decisions and go their own way. I think he would have been happy to have his story described as an ordinary story of a man who was trustworthy, but to be the subject of a narrative in history would never do. It is his actions that live, and so I write under the umbrella of his life.

# The Speech of Angels

*After reading an article on Dante's Treatise on Language*

Shifts of language

Clumsy floating variables
To share the totality of nature
And the stuff of heaven
The interference and
Meddling gossip of media
Hurl pillows and panic
Congregations of prime-time cannibals
Selling pharmaceuticals

The circus improbability
Of pageant winners
Defined as statesmen
Preach solemnly with
Thick lips and slender hands
There is no greater eloquence
Or compelling cognitive thunder
Than the unspoken visions of the dead

We shared our touch

And now it is more

A promenade through burden and joy
A triumph of life via death
Where the designs of our natural world
Flower
Not in inexpensive words
But sacred bouquets of silence
Our speech in thought and vision
Forever defined and everlasting in the now
And the success of this perfect language
Transformed to the sharing of infinity

I see Nonno with his grey vest
And white t-shirt
Why does he smile and not laugh
To the little boy looking up?
His angel assures and articulates
His heart in mine
I become the answer to every young riddle
That surrounds the bewilderment of a child
His silence is not obscure
And it is not finite
It is sweet and shatters complications

In early growing days
I shared a hard firmament
With Mama and Papá
Scraped and suffered necessary treaties
Endured the venue of voice
And were prejudiced by its sound

Near their corporal ends
The material world
Changed the rules of speech
To terrible and hurtful noises
But the unmistakable dialogue
Of their newer angels
Rescued me from pain and delivered us
To a pact of acceptance in simplicity of love

Now I talk to Mama
She tells me Giulio I was not afraid
You saw the cancer mask my face
It cannot interfere with us now
Or forevermore
Papá's angel does not have tremors
He still shaves with a straight razor
Has a garden that everyone admires
He speaks as before in stuttering excitement
And I am glad as these are his ways
I recognize my beloved father
When he explains to his friends
"This is my son"

In absence they are not silent
I cannot miss my angels
And they cannot miss me
Find your angels
For they have been waiting
And wait for you still

# She was too Young to Know Any Better She Called Him Little Friend

Little Barbara didn't know any better, but she didn't know she knew everything. She would hold Little Friend and have conversations. He would want to know what she thought and she would tell him. They got along famously, this little stuffed elephant, and Barbara. The little stuffed toy looked like an ordinary plush animal to others, but Barbara called him Little Friend. They supposed that Barbara was attached to it because of the large floppy ears. She was thought to be a compassionate child. Barbara was careful to hold him tenderly, and stare at Little Friend's face, because they were having a private conversation. When she addressed him, she embraced him gently and crumpled her eyes in his, as she knew he did when he spoke to her. They are the deepest of friends, and share their secrets together, but it is okay, as long as Barbara does her chores and behaves. There was no acting out when Barbara was young, so it was a good life for her and Little Friend. Sometimes others in the family would tell her to do something other than be with her beloved partner. They observed that her time with Little Friend was too much. But Barbara knew better. She took Little Friend to solitary, alone places, and explained. They would have their talks, which did a lot of good for both of them. It taught them how to deal with the problems of those who could not understand kindness. Like many kids little Barbara at five years old had a doctorate in kindness. Her practice was the kitchen table, bed, and front porch. Little Friend and she would have their talks and clarify all of it. They had a secret gift of good luck that they shared whenever they were together, but they had to face each other for it to work. Theirs was a harmony in two parts. One was the voice of little Barbara, and the other was the wonderful voice of Little Friend, the creation of this wondrous girl who became the woman Barbara, now my wife. She kept the kindness, and it has grown in her and is now shared with me. I look around and want to thank Little Friend for all he has done for us... I cannot find him, but he is here inside her heart, and now ours.

# La Cara Ragazzazina Toscana

Molti anni fa ho incontrato una ragazzina in una piccola città... Era Chiesina Uzzanese in Toscana, la città di mio Nonno.

Many years ago I met a young girl in a small town... It was Chiesina Uzzanese in Toscana, the town of my grandfather. One of her favorite things was to laugh at me when I spoke, and to look at my shoes. That seemed to be all she needed to capture my heart. Ma sei fuori! No, not crazy. And my feet can breathe. The shoes do not choke them. Come ti chiami? Mi chiama Fiorella, ma Fia in breve. I am called Fiorella but Fia for short. She took me by the hand and led me to the side of the road. She picked a flower on the path and handed it to me and said, "Sono il piccolo fiore e tu mi tieni in mano!" "I am the little flower and you hold me in your hand!" She laughed and ran in what looked like a brown uniform created for this child of Toscana. Perhaps it was a birthright of her village? It did not complement her disheveled auburn hair. She knew the mischievous intent of her smile and the magic of her eyes. How can one so young and small understand the greater subtleties of living? This is Chiesina Uzzanese, not New York.

She quietly took my hand and we began walking on the Strada Senza Nome. Street Without a Name. She explained that her parents had a farm there, and that she had a brother and sister. By this time, I had also taken off my shoes and socks, to her great delight. She had tied one of the socks around her hair to show her Mama.

As we approached the farm I was surprised at the size of the place. Definitely old, but a large farm with a moderate sized house and barn. Fia led me directly to the barn. It appeared she was more excited for me to meet the animals than her family, which is typical of kids everywhere. There were chickens, a few goats, and a horse in a stable.

There were at least three dogs, all mutts running around that wanted to play with Fia, and examine my credentials. Fia, of course, had to formally introduce us. "Giulio, quest' è Luca" She presented the dogs to us one by one, as if in court. "Piacere di conoscerti Luca!" Pleased to meet you, Luca, and so with all the rest... Fia took her responsibilities as hostess seriously, but behind it all I could tell she thoroughly enjoyed her young role as a Signora. But what other responsibilities await young Fia? At this time a signora was the role she saw, but this bare-footed contessa was being groomed for much more than the wife and mother of a neighboring Toscano. It was obvious that Fia was an extraordinary child. Here she was in her little brown garb and scruffy hair, conquering this curious Italian American from Pittsburgh.

"Dov'è la mamma?" Where is Mamma? "La mamma è a casa. Ti prenderò" Mamma is at the house. I will take you. Again, hand in hand we went towards the house. There was a seperate entry for the kitchen, which seemed like the main entrance to the house. "Mamma vieni a conoscere la mia nuova amica!" Mamma come and meet my new friend! A woman approached from the next room and grinned politely with anticipation. "Buon giorno, Signora..." It occurred to me that I did not know Fia's last name. I simply said defensively Mi chiamo Giulio Magrini. Piacere di conoscerla, signora. Mi scusa, non conosco il cognome di Fia... "Il nostro cognome è Lupori" Our last name is Lupori.

My mind started to whirr with excitement. On October 12, 1901, my Nonno boarded the S.S. L' Aquitaine at Le Havre and landed in New York October 19, 1901, bound for Pittsburgh. He was fourteen, with $10.00 in his pocket. On the ship manifest it showed he had departed from Chiesina Uzzanese. Accompanying with him were two other passengers, also from Chiesina Uzzanese. Franco and Ginevra Lupori, both 26. All were bound for Pittsburgh.

Signora Lupori asked if I wanted an espresso. "No grazie faceva troppo caldo ma un po' d'acqua è buona" No thanks, it was too hot a day, but a little water would be good. I asked her if she had any older relatives. I told her the story of Franco and Ginerva Lupori. At this time, Fia, who had been listening intently to my story, asked about my Nonno. Why did he leave his home to go to America? Fia was not yet fourteen, but said she would never leave even little Luca for anywhere. I told her he is a wonderful dog, but sometimes even when a person is young there is something inside that tells him or her that they have to follow another road. Maybe Nonno heard a voice when he was fourteen in Chiesina Uzzanese. There are many voices to be heard everywhere. We must always listen to them. They will never lie to us. For some the voices tell us to leave. For others the voices tell us stay. We must always respect our own voices and the choices of others.

I never saw Fia or her Mamma again. My heart aches for her. I wonder what she did with her life. I will not permit myself to be sad about her choices. If she is a professional of some kind with a career or a housewife it will not matter. Her choice and her happiness matter. The bare-footed joy she shared with me on a Tuscan road mattered. If she could do that with me for part of a day, I knew she could do anything with anyone her entire life. I never found out about other Lupori's who ventured to America with Nonno Giulio Magrini. I carry him with me in my heart, with many others, perhaps- not enough. Fia's lesson taught me that there is room in my heart for more.

# Selinsgrove Dark

*A recollection on the life and death of my sister Diane Louise Magrini who had Down Syndrome, and was institutionalized around 1951. She died 10/18/72, and was 21 years old. She lived in Selingsgrove PA. In those days many children stayed at such institutions. She had her local parents in the Selinsgrove area, and we traveled to visit as often as possible. The institution did not make a good impression on me.*

selinsgrove DARK
again and again
only for the children
the kids the little ones the
DARKNESS

in the eyes of the nurses
the pockets of the doctors DARK
in the policy
of the administrative staff DARKNESS

clings to the braces the crutches
the amazing patience of the therapists DARK
in the comfort of eternal linoleum plotting the
DARK
paths down the wells DARKNESS

in the strokes
of the washer woman's mop the
DARK
predators in her bucket
the faded clowns and giraffes the
DARKNESS
Of the broken blond doll in the crayon box and

DARKNESS too
in play TIME
and supper TIME
and nap TIME

DARKNESS
fading fading
DARKNESS
in the wasting away
of hide and go seek Joey and Annie
with the almond eyes

DARKNESS
in the parade
of mommys and daddys
stepping politely through the urine

why
my daughter why her
why
my son why him
and the money piles and piles DARKNESS

every year every
year
DARKNESS
it comes
oh it comes

Diane

don't go

and selinsgrove
DARK
is
BLACK now
as
BLACK
as
BLACK
as
BLACK
as

sssssssssssssshhhh

**(as a lullabye)**

bye-lo baby bye-lo baby bye-lo baby
bye-lo baby bye
mommy still loves you mommy still loves you mommy still
loves you
though you've gone away

# For All My Days Remaining

*Written when I retired, now broader applications exist*

You, now me

Offered the blessings
Of the dust and brick

My small hands held in yours
Now holds another
To guide uncertain steps
Passing the wand of strength
To sticky hands that reach from below

My compass is engaged
The North Star is fixed
And so am I

I am the radiant light of the universe
The unconsumed burning
Not in testament
But in blood

The face of a father
Eliminates fear
Or at least
Until fear is fed by time
And now I am aged
And they say I am an empty warrior

The conflicts of today
Do not attend to me
It is whispered I am weak and weathered
Not a worthy opponent
For the fear of life or the life of fear
The moments stand ready to punish me

LET    US    SHARE    THE    ENLIGHTENMENT

I travail the gloaming
Leap through barricades
I emerge
And break victorious
Through the eras of our age

I do not hear
The trembling voice of weary
Plummet from my wits
Through my promenade of words
Marching forward

I am told
These pounding waves of days
Debilitate and weaken the spirit
Through natural regressions and decay

Who are these people
And who do they pray to?

I am here tonight to say
I am veracity
The exemplification of protest
My conflict and victories

Whet my appetite for more
My aging cause
Battles with nobility
And develops an unshakable strength
And I will not be stopped

I supernova through time
There is no defeat in me
My heart radiates love with every beat
And for all my days remaining
I will rapture
In these heavens
I will define the life I lead
For all my days remaining

# The Revelation of Her Embrace

When I was a small boy
I played in the Sharpsburg mud
I decided it would be a good idea
To kiss my mother

She was doing the wash
By hand
In the back yard

I pulled at her dress
She picked me up
And kissed me
She didn't mind
My muddy hands
Over her clean white dress

Today my heart beats
In remembrance of those days
And the memory and wonder
Lifts me still
To a never-ending resurrection

Her love conquers the mud of eternity
In these years she has never let me go
All I need to do is remember
And I am safe in her arms

# The Color of Dirt Afterword

The essence of the dirt beneath enhances our spirits. The characteristics through infinity have shaped our lives and shaken history. The symmetry of the dirt and those who traverse it are intrinsically bound. The fields sustain us, and will punish when we are preoccupied. The stains of our charges accumulate upon it, and we abide or perish together. We collaborate victory and failure and embrace the sum of our existence for what we have produced.

We tell ourselves fables and present dogma regarding the leavings and production of the color of dirt. Some take the stories and create inflexible laws that may not be broken or questioned. They draw intractable lines through the color of dirt and tenets of life with their philosophy of the meaning of dirt. For them their principles of dirt in their present are their principles of dirt in eternity. I was taught another way. The life I have known has always depended on the tangible function of dirt. I needed to depend on the palpable resource of dirt to draw on its power, to collaborate with its substance. For us there was no spiritual dirt, no faux resource existing to support frailty. We are partners, and define each other equally.

This discussion of dirt has fractured into a cultural morass analyzing the effect of the groups that walk upon it. They tend to want to personalize their dirt. I have seen the preposterous waddling of their steps. They attempt to categorize dirt, which is the same dirt everywhere for everyone. When others trod on the same dirt they assert the dirt changes, or worse... The dirt is made more worthy by their steps.

We carry our value ourselves and work with the dirt in solidarity. We cannot appraise external value. All merit flows from the outside to its internal home. Embrace and grow with your partners. Reject those who would sever you from your place. We have put our hands in the dirt and sanctified each other.

WA

www.ingramcontent.com/pod-product-compliance
Lightning Source LLC
Chambersburg PA
CBHW061604110426
42742CB00039B/2770